Cookies Cookbook

By Jane Biondi

Copyright © 2015 by Jane Biondi.

All legal rights reserved. You cannot offer this book for free or sell it. You do not have reselling legal rights to this book. This eBook may not be recreated in any file format or physical format without having the expressed written approval of Jane Biondi. All Violators will be sued.

While efforts have been made to assess that the information contained in this book is valid, neither the author nor the publisher assumes any accountability for errors, interpretations, omissions or usage of the subject matters herein.

Disclaimer:

The Information presented in this book is created to provide useful information on the subject areas discussed. The publisher and author are not accountable for any particular health or allergic reaction needs that may involve medical supervision and are not liable for any damage or damaging outcomes from any treatment, application or preparation, action, to any person reading or adhering to the information in this book. References are presented for informational reasons only and do not represent an endorsement of any web sites or other sources. Audience should be informed that the websites mentioned in this book may change.

This publication includes opinions and ideas of its author and is meant for informational purposes only. The author and publisher shall in no event be held liable for any damage or loss sustained from the usage of this publication.

Table of Contents

Cookies Cookbook 1
   Introduction 4
Cookies Recipes 5
   Chocolate Chip Cookies 5
   M&M Cookies 6
   Coconut Pecan Cookies 7
   Double Chocolate Chip Cookies 8
   Macadamia Cookies 9
   Biscotti 11
   Black Forest Cookies 12
   Almond Cookies 14
   Smiling Cashew Cookies 15
   Honey Heart Cookies 16
   Sesame Cookies 17
   Walnut Thumbprint Cookies 19
   Peanut Butter Chocolate Kisses 21
   Peanut Butter Peanut Cookies 22
   Macadamia Cookies 24
   Lemon Wedding Cookies 25
   Yellow, Green & Pink French Macarons 26
   Italian Amaretto Cookies 28
   Cannoli 29
   Oatmeal Raisin Cookies 31
   Coconut Macaroons 33

Anise & Coconut Cookies 34

Pizzelle 35

Almond Anise Star Cookies 35

Black Sesame Cookies 37

Waffle Cookies 38

Rolled Pizzelle 39

Italian Hazelnut Cookies 41

Almond Slivers Cookies 42

Gingerbread cookies 43

Introduction

Hello,

My name is Jane Biondi and as every Italian, I'm a huge fan of Italian cuisine. My previous books were dedicated to healthy Pasta and Pasta salads, but this one is dedicated to Italian cookies.

Most of the recipes are for 30 cookies. Bake them until hard around the edges but still soft in the middle. Enjoy!!!

Cookies Recipes
Chocolate Chip Cookies

Yields 30 cookies

Ingredients:
2 + 1/2 cup all-purpose flour
1 + 1/2 cup brown sugar or powdered sugar
1/2 tsp. baking soda
2 sticks chopped unsalted butter at room temperature
2 large eggs
1/2 tsp. salt
2 tsp. vanilla extract
2 cups chocolate chips

Baking Instructions: Preheat oven to 375f. Beat butter and sugar until light and fluffy and beat in eggs one at a time. Mix all dry ingredients in fairly large mixing bowl. Add dry ingredients until well mixed. Add vanilla and chocolate chips and stir. Line the baking sheet and drop large tablespoons of dough 2 inch apart and bake for 10-12 minutes for chewy and 14-16 minutes for crunchy cookies.

M&M Cookies
Yields 30 cookies

Ingredients:
2 + 1/2 cup all-purpose flour
1 + 1/2 cup brown sugar or powdered sugar
1/2 tsp. baking soda
2 sticks chopped unsalted butter at room temperature
2 large eggs
1/2 tsp. salt
2 tsp. vanilla extract
2 cups m&m's

Baking Instructions: Preheat oven to 375f. Beat butter and sugar until light and fluffy and beat in eggs one at a time. Mix all dry ingredients in fairly large mixing bowl. Add dry ingredients until well mixed. Add vanilla and m&m's and stir. Line the baking sheet and drop large tablespoons of dough 2 inch apart and bake for 10-12 minutes for chewy and 14-16 minutes for crunchy cookies.

Coconut Pecan Cookies
Yields 30 cookies

Ingredients:
2 + 1/2 cup all-purpose flour
1 + 1/2 cup brown sugar or powdered sugar
1/2 tsp. baking soda
2 sticks chopped unsalted butter at room temperature
2 large eggs
1/2 tsp. salt
2 tsp. vanilla extract
1 cup chopped pecans
1 cup shredded coconut

Baking Instructions: Preheat oven to 375f. Beat butter and sugar until light and fluffy and beat in eggs one at a time. Mix all dry ingredients in fairly large mixing bowl. Add dry ingredients until well mixed. Add vanilla, pecans and coconut and stir. Line the baking sheet and drop large tablespoons of dough 2 inch apart and bake for 10-12 minutes for chewy and 14-16 minutes for crunchy cookies.

Double Chocolate Chip Cookies
Yields 30 cookies

Ingredients:
2 + 1/2 cup all-purpose flour
1 + 1/2 cup brown sugar or powdered sugar
1/2 tsp. baking soda
3/4 cup unsweetened cocoa
2 sticks chopped unsalted butter at room temperature
2 large eggs
1/2 tsp. salt
2 tsp. vanilla extract
2 cups chocolate chips

Baking Instructions: Preheat oven to 375f. Beat butter and sugar until light and fluffy and beat in eggs one at a time. Mix all dry ingredients in fairly large mixing bowl. Add dry ingredients until well mixed. Add vanilla and chocolate chips and stir. Line the baking sheet and drop large tablespoons of dough 2 inch apart and bake for 10-12 minutes for chewy and 14-16 minutes for crunchy cookies.

Macadamia Cookies

Yields 30 cookies

Ingredients:
2 + 1/2 cup all-purpose flour
1 + 1/2 cup brown sugar or powdered sugar
1/2 tsp. baking soda
2 sticks chopped unsalted butter at room temperature
2 large eggs
1/2 tsp. salt
2 tsp. vanilla extract
1 cup chopped macadamia nuts
1 cup halved macadamia nuts – for decoration

Baking Instructions: Preheat oven to 375f. Beat butter and sugar until light and fluffy and beat in eggs one at a time. Mix all dry ingredients in fairly large mixing bowl. Add dry ingredients until well mixed. Add vanilla and chopped macadamia nuts and stir. Line the baking sheet and drop large tablespoons of dough 2 inch apart, decorate with macadamia nuts halves and bake for 10-12 minutes for chewy and 14-16 minutes for crunchy cookies.

Biscotti

Yields 30 cookies

Ingredients:
2 + 1/2 cup all-purpose flour
1 cup white sugar or powdered sugar
1/2 tsp. baking soda
1 stick chopped unsalted butter at room temperature
3 large eggs
1/2 tsp. salt
2 tsp. almond extract
1 cup chopped almonds

Baking Instructions: Preheat oven to 375f. Beat butter and sugar until light and fluffy and beat in eggs one at a time. Mix all dry ingredients in fairly large mixing bowl. Add dry ingredients until well mixed. Add almond extract and almond and stir. Line the baking sheet and divide the dough into 2 parts (as long as the cooking sheet, 1/2 inch high) and bake for 30 minutes. Cool and slice into 1/2 inch slices and bake on each side for 5-10 more minutes.

Black Forest Cookies

Yields 30 cookies

Ingredients:
2 + 1/2 cup all-purpose flour
1 + 1/2 cup brown sugar or powdered sugar
1/2 tsp. baking soda
2 sticks chopped unsalted butter at room temperature
2 large eggs
1/2 tsp. salt
2 tsp. vanilla extract

Baking Instructions: Preheat oven to 375f. Beat butter and sugar until light and fluffy and beat in eggs one at a time. Mix all dry ingredients in fairly large mixing bowl. Add dry ingredients until well mixed. Add vanilla and stir. Line the baking sheet and drop large tablespoons of dough 2 inch apart and bake for 10-12 minutes for chewy and 14-16 minutes for crunchy cookies.

Buttercream Frosting Ingredients:
2 sticks chopped unsalted butter at room temperature
3 cups powdered sugar
1 tsp. vanilla extract
2 cups cherry preserve

Buttercream Instructions:

Beat the butter for few minutes and start adding sugar until light and fluffy and mix in vanilla until incorporated. Put a teaspoon of cream on top of each cookies and teaspoon of cherry preserve.

Almond Cookies

Yields 30 cookies

Ingredients:
2 + 1/2 cup all-purpose flour
1 + 1/2 cup brown sugar or powdered sugar
1/2 tsp. baking soda
2 sticks chopped unsalted butter at room temperature
2 large eggs
1/2 tsp. salt
2 tsp. almond extract
1 cup chopped almonds + 30 whole almonds for decoration.

Baking Instructions: Preheat oven to 375f. Beat butter and sugar until light and fluffy and beat in eggs one at a time. Mix all dry ingredients in fairly large mixing bowl. Add dry ingredients until well mixed. Add almond extract and chopped almonds and stir. Line the baking sheet and drop large tablespoons of dough 2 inch apart, press whole almond into each cookie and bake for 10-12 minutes for chewy and 14-16 minutes for crunchy cookies.

Smiling Cashew Cookies

Yields 30 cookies

Ingredients:
2 + 1/2 cup all-purpose flour
1 + 1/2 cup brown sugar or powdered sugar
1/2 tsp. baking soda
2 sticks chopped unsalted butter at room temperature
2 large eggs
1/2 tsp. salt
2 tsp. vanilla extract
1 cup whole cashews
1/2 cup small chocolate chips for decoration

Baking Instructions: Preheat oven to 375f. Beat butter and sugar until light and fluffy and beat in eggs one at a time. Mix all dry ingredients in fairly large mixing bowl. Add dry ingredients until well mixed. Add vanilla and stir. Line the baking sheet and drop large tablespoons of dough 2 inch apart, decorate with cashews as lips and chocolate chips as eyes (see picture) and bake for 10-12 minutes for chewy and 14-16 minutes for crunchy cookies.

Honey Heart Cookies

Yields 30 cookies

Ingredients:
2 + 1/2 cup all-purpose flour
1/2 cup brown sugar or powdered sugar
1/2 cup honey
1/2 tsp. baking soda
2 sticks chopped unsalted butter at room temperature
2 large eggs
1/2 tsp. salt
1/2 tsp. ground cinnamon
1/4 tsp. ground cloves

Baking Instructions: Preheat oven to 375f. Beat butter, honey and sugar until light and fluffy and beat in eggs one at a time. Mix all dry ingredients in fairly large mixing bowl. Add dry ingredients until well mixed. Line the baking sheet and drop large tablespoons of dough 2 inch apart and bake for 10-12 minutes for chewy and 14-16 minutes for crunchy cookies.

Sesame Cookies
Yields 30 cookies

Ingredients:
2 + 1/2 cup all-purpose flour
1 + 1/2 cup brown sugar or powdered sugar
1/2 tsp. baking soda
2 sticks chopped unsalted butter at room temperature
2 large eggs
1/2 tsp. salt
2 tsp. anise extract
1 cup sesame seeds

Baking Instructions: Preheat oven to 375f. Beat butter and sugar until light and fluffy and beat in eggs one at a time. Mix all dry ingredients in fairly large mixing bowl. Add dry ingredients until well mixed. Add anise and stir. Line the baking sheet and drop large tablespoons of dough 2 inch apart, sprinkle with sesame seeds and bake for 10-12 minutes for chewy and 14-16 minutes for crunchy cookies.

Walnut Thumbprint Cookies

Yields 30 cookies

Ingredients:
2 + 1/2 cup all-purpose flour
1 + 1/2 cup brown sugar or powdered sugar
1/2 tsp. baking soda
2 sticks chopped unsalted butter at room temperature
2 large eggs
1/2 tsp. salt
2 tsp. vanilla extract
2 cup chopped walnuts (one for dough and 1 for sprinkling)
1 cup raspberry preserve

Baking Instructions: Preheat oven to 375f. Beat butter and sugar until light and fluffy and beat in eggs one at a time. Mix all dry ingredients in fairly large mixing bowl. Add dry ingredients until well mixed. Add vanilla and 1 cup chopped walnuts and stir. Line the baking sheet, shape dough into balls, roll them in walnuts, arrange them 2 inch apart and press slightly in the center. Spoon a little bit of preserve in the center and bake for 10-12 minutes for chewy and 14-16 minutes for crunchy cookies.

Peanut Butter Chocolate Kisses

Yields 30 cookies

Ingredients:
2 + 1/2 cup all-purpose flour
1 + 1/2 cup brown sugar or powdered sugar
1/2 tsp. baking soda
2 sticks chopped unsalted butter at room temperature
2 large eggs
1/2 tsp. salt
2 tsp. vanilla extract
30 Hershey kisses

Baking Instructions: Preheat oven to 375f. Beat butter and sugar until light and fluffy and beat in eggs one at a time. Mix all dry ingredients in fairly large mixing bowl. Add dry ingredients until well mixed. Add vanilla and stir. Line the baking sheet and drop large tablespoons of dough 2 inch apart, dent with the thumb in the middle and bake for 10 minutes. Press the chocolate into the cookies right after the baking.

Peanut Butter Peanut Cookies

Yields 30 cookies

Ingredients:
2 + 1/2 cup all-purpose flour
1 + 1/2 cup brown sugar or powdered sugar
1/2 tsp. baking soda
1 stick chopped unsalted butter at room temperature
2 large eggs
1/2 tsp. salt
2 tsp. vanilla extract
1 cup peanut butter
1/2 cup chopped peanuts

Baking Instructions: Preheat oven to 375f. Beat butter and sugar until light and fluffy and beat in eggs one at a time. Mix all dry ingredients in fairly large mixing bowl. Add dry ingredients until well mixed. Add vanilla, peanut butter and chopped peanuts and stir. Line the baking sheet and drop large tablespoons of dough 2 inch apart and bake for 10-12 minutes for chewy and 14-16 minutes for crunchy cookies.

Macadamia Cookies
Yields 30 cookies

Ingredients:
2 + 1/2 cup all-purpose flour
1 + 1/2 cup brown sugar or powdered sugar
1/2 tsp. baking soda
2 sticks chopped unsalted butter at room temperature
2 large eggs
1/2 tsp. salt
2 tsp. vanilla extract
1 cup chopped macadamia nuts

Baking Instructions: Preheat oven to 375f. Beat butter and sugar until light and fluffy and beat in eggs one at a time. Mix all dry ingredients in fairly large mixing bowl. Add dry ingredients until well mixed. Add vanilla and macadamia nuts and stir. Line the baking sheet and drop large tablespoons of dough 2 inch apart and bake for 10-12 minutes for chewy and 14-16 minutes for crunchy cookies.

Lemon Wedding Cookies

Yields 30 cookies

Ingredients:
2 + 1/2 cup all-purpose flour
1 + 1/2 cup powdered sugar (1/2 cup for dusting)
1/2 tsp. baking soda
2 sticks chopped unsalted butter at room temperature
2 large eggs
1/2 tsp. salt
2 tsp. vanilla extract
1 package of lemon instant pudding mix (3.4 oz.)
1 tsp. lemon zest

Baking Instructions: Preheat oven to 375f. Beat butter and 1 cup sugar until light and fluffy and beat in eggs one at a time. Mix all dry ingredients in fairly large mixing bowl. Add dry ingredients until well mixed. Add vanilla and stir. Line the baking sheet and drop large tablespoons of dough 2 inch apart and bake for 10-12 minutes for chewy and 14-16 minutes for crunchy cookies.

Yellow, Green & Pink French Macarons

Yields 30 cookies

Ingredients:
1 cup almond flour
1 + 3/4 cup powdered sugar
3 tbsp. white sugar
3 large egg whites
Pinch of salt
2-3 drops food coloring
1/2 tsp. vanilla or almond extract

Baking Instructions: Preheat oven to 290f. Mix powdered sugar and almond in fairly large mixing bowl. Beat eggs until foamy. Beat in salt and white sugar until fluffy. Gently fold in dry ingredients, food coloring and extract in until well mixed. Let the batter sit for 20 minutes. Line the baking sheet with silicone baking mats and fill the piping bag. Pipe 2 inch discs 2 inch apart and let sit for an hour. Bake for 10 minutes. Cool before filling

Buttercream Frosting Ingredients:
2 sticks chopped unsalted butter at room temperature
3 cups powdered sugar
1 tsp. vanilla extract

Buttercream Instructions:

Beat the butter for few minutes and start adding sugar until light and fluffy and mix in vanilla until incorporated. Fill and sandwich macarons.

Italian Amaretto Cookies

Yields 30 cookies

Ingredients:
2 + 1/2 cup all-purpose flour
1 + 1/2 cup brown sugar or powdered sugar
1/2 tsp. baking soda
2 sticks chopped unsalted butter at room temperature
2 large eggs
1/2 tsp. salt
2 tsp. almond extract
1 cup chopped almonds

Baking Instructions: Preheat oven to 375f. Beat butter and sugar until light and fluffy and beat in eggs one at a time. Mix all dry ingredients in fairly large mixing bowl. Add dry ingredients until well mixed. Add almond extract and chopped almonds and stir. Line the baking sheet , fill piping bag and pipi 2 inch swirls 2 inch apart, decorate with sprinkles of choice and bake for 10-12 minutes for chewy and 14-16 minutes for crunchy cookies.

Cannoli

Yields 30 cookies

Ingredients:
2 + 1/2 cup all-purpose flour
1/4 cup sugar
1/2 cup white wine
3 Tbsp. butter at room temperature
1 egg + 1 egg yolk
1/4 tsp. salt
2 tsp. vanilla extract
1 egg white for sealing the cannoli
Powdered sugar for dusting
Oil for frying

Baking Instructions: Beat butter and sugar until light and fluffy and beat in eggs one at a time. Mix all dry ingredients in fairly large mixing bowl. Add dry ingredients and wine and mix until well mixed. Cover the dough and refrigerate for 1-2 hours. Take it out and let sit until it reaches room temperature. Dust the dough with flour and roll it through pasta machine (pick the thickest setting). In the meantime, heat the oil in the heavy skillet or deep fryer. Place the dough on a lightly dusted surface and with a 4 inch diameter glass cut circles. Roll the dough around cannoli mold and seal with egg white. Hold the mold with thongs and fry each cannoli for few minutes until crispy. Carefully slide cannoli off the mold (use kitchen towel and twist them a little bit) and let cool. Repeat for the rest of the dough.

Filling Ingredients:
2 cups ricotta
2/3 cups sugar
1/4 tsp. ground cinnamon or lemon zest

Filling Instructions:

Mix ricotta, sugar and cinnamon. Fill the piping bag and pipe the filling in cannoli.

Oatmeal Raisin Cookies

Ingredients

- 1 cup coconut oil
- 1 cup coconut sugar. Other option is raw honey
- 1 1/2 cups almond flour
- 1 teaspoon salt
- 1/2 teaspoon grated nutmeg
- 1 teaspoon cinnamon
- 1 1/2 cups raisins
- 2 large eggs, well beaten
- 1 Tbsp. ground vanilla bean
- 3 cups rolled oats
- 1/2 cup chopped walnuts

Instructions

Heat oven to 350 F. Grease cookie sheets with coconut oil or line with waxed or parchment paper. Mix coconut oil, coconut sugar or raw honey in a large bowl and beat until fluffy. Add vanilla. Then beat in eggs. Mix almond flour, salt, cinnamon, and nutmeg in a separate bowl. Stir these dry ingredients into fluffy mixture. Mix in raisins and nuts. Mix in oats. Spoon out on cookie sheets, leaving 2 inches between cookies. Bake until edges turn golden brown.

Coconut Macaroons

Ingredients

- 12 egg whites
- 2 cup coconut sugar
- 1/2 tsp. salt
- 3 cups unsweetened flaked coconut

Heat the oven to 325 degrees. Whisk together egg whites, sugar, and salt in a bowl until frothy. Add coconut and mix to combine.

Shape mixture into mounds with hands and place one inch apart on baking sheet.

Bake until lightly golden, 35 to 40 minutes. Rotate sheet halfway through.

Anise & Coconut Cookies

Yields 30 cookies

Ingredients:
2 + 1/2 cup all-purpose flour
1 + 1/2 cup brown sugar or powdered sugar
1/2 tsp. baking soda
2 sticks chopped unsalted butter at room temperature
2 large eggs
1/2 tsp. salt
2 tsp. anise extract
1 cup shredded coconut

Baking Instructions: Preheat oven to 375f. Beat butter and sugar until light and fluffy and beat in eggs one at a time. Mix all dry ingredients in fairly large mixing bowl. Add dry ingredients until well mixed. Add anise and coconut and stir. Line the baking sheet and drop large tablespoons of dough 2 inch apart and bake for 10-12 minutes for chewy and 14-16 minutes for crunchy cookies.

Pizzelle

Yields 30 cookies

Ingredients:
2 + 1/2 cup all-purpose flour
1 + 1/2 cup powdered sugar (1/2 half for dusting)
1/2 tsp. baking soda
2 sticks chopped unsalted butter at room temperature
4 large eggs
1/2 tsp. salt
2 tsp. vanilla and optional anise extract

Baking Instructions: You'll need pizzelle iron. Beat butter and 1 cup sugar until light and fluffy and beat in eggs one at a time. Mix all dry ingredients in fairly large mixing bowl. Add dry ingredients until well mixed. Add vanilla and anise and stir. Heat pizzelle iron and drop large tablespoons of dough, close the lid and bake for 30 seconds. Dust with powdered sugar.

Almond Anise Star Cookies

Yields 30 cookies

Ingredients:
2 + 1/2 cup all-purpose flour
1 + 1/2 cup brown sugar or powdered sugar
1/2 tsp. baking soda
2 sticks chopped unsalted butter at room temperature
2 large eggs
1/2 tsp. salt
2 tsp. almond extract
2 tsp. anise extract
1 cup powdered sugar for dusting

Baking Instructions: Preheat oven to 375f. Beat butter and sugar until light and fluffy and beat in eggs one at a time. Mix all dry ingredients in fairly large mixing bowl. Add dry ingredients until well mixed. Add almond and anise extract and stir. Line the baking sheet, roll the dough and use star shaped cookie cutters. Place cookies 2 inch apart and bake for 10-12 minutes for chewy and 14-16 minutes for crunchy cookies. Dust with powdered sugar.

Black Sesame Cookies

Yields 30 cookies

Ingredients:
2 + 1/2 cup all-purpose flour
1 + 1/2 cup brown sugar or powdered sugar
1/2 tsp. baking soda
2 sticks chopped unsalted butter at room temperature
2 large eggs
1/2 tsp. salt
2 tsp. vanilla extract
1 cup black sesame seeds

Baking Instructions: Preheat oven to 375f. Beat butter and sugar until light and fluffy and beat in eggs one at a time. Mix all dry ingredients in fairly large mixing bowl. Add dry ingredients until well mixed. Add vanilla and stir. Line the baking sheet and drop large tablespoons of dough 2 inch apart, sprinkle with black sesame seeds and bake for 10-12 minutes for chewy and 14-16 minutes for crunchy cookies.

Waffle Cookies

Yields 10 waffles

Ingredients:
2 cups all-purpose flour
3/4 cup brown sugar or powdered sugar
1 tsp. baking soda
2 sticks chopped unsalted butter at room temperature
2 large eggs, separated
1 tsp. vanilla extract
1 + 1/2 cups milk

Baking Instructions: Preheat oven to 375f. Beat egg yolks, and add butter, milk and vanilla. Mix all dry ingredients in fairly large mixing bowl. Add dry ingredients to yolk and butter mixture and mix. Beat egg whites until peaks form and fold in the mixture. Bake in the preheated waffle iron.

Rolled Pizzelle

Yields 30 cookies

Ingredients:
2 + 1/2 cup all-purpose flour
1 + 1/2 cup powdered sugar (1/2 half for dusting)
1/2 tsp. baking soda
2 sticks chopped unsalted butter at room temperature
4 large eggs
1/2 tsp. salt
2 tsp. vanilla and optional anise extract

Baking Instructions: You'll need pizzelle iron and some cleaned markers for rolling pizzelles around them. Beat butter and 1 cup sugar until light and fluffy and beat in eggs one at a time. Mix all dry ingredients in fairly large mixing bowl. Add dry ingredients until well mixed. Add vanilla and anise and stir. Heat pizzelle iron and drop large tablespoons of dough, close the lid and bake for 30 seconds. Take the pizzelle out and roll it right away around marker. If they cool, they will become too stiff to be rolled around. Repeat with all the batter.

Buttercream Frosting Ingredients:
2 sticks chopped unsalted butter at room temperature
3 cups powdered sugar
1 tsp. vanilla extract

Buttercream Instructions:

Beat the butter for few minutes and start adding sugar until light and fluffy and mix in vanilla until incorporated. Fill the piping bag and fill pizzelles.

Italian Hazelnut Cookies

Yields 30 cookies

Ingredients:
2 + 1/2 cup all-purpose flour
1 + 1/2 cup brown sugar or powdered sugar
1/2 tsp. baking soda
2 sticks chopped unsalted butter at room temperature
2 large eggs
1/2 tsp. salt
2 tsp. vanilla extract
1 cup chopped hazelnuts

Baking Instructions: Preheat oven to 375f. Beat butter and sugar until light and fluffy and beat in eggs one at a time. Mix all dry ingredients in fairly large mixing bowl. Add dry ingredients until well mixed. Add vanilla and hazelnuts and stir. Line the baking sheet and drop large tablespoons of dough 2 inch apart and bake for 10-12 minutes for chewy and 14-16 minutes for crunchy cookies.

Almond Slivers Cookies

Yields 30 cookies

Ingredients:
2 + 1/2 cup all-purpose flour
1 + 1/2 cup brown sugar or powdered sugar
1/2 tsp. baking soda
2 sticks chopped unsalted butter at room temperature
2 large eggs
1/2 tsp. salt
2 tsp. almond extract
1 cup chopped almond and 1 cup almond slivers

Baking Instructions: Preheat oven to 375f. Beat butter and sugar until light and fluffy and beat in eggs one at a time. Mix all dry ingredients in fairly large mixing bowl. Add dry ingredients until well mixed. Add almond extract and chopped almonds and stir. Line the baking sheet and drop large tablespoons of dough in the bowl with almond slivers, roll them in slivers and place 2 inch apart on the baking sheet. Bake for 10-12 minutes for chewy and 14-16 minutes for crunchy cookies.

Gingerbread cookies

Yields 30 cookies

Ingredients:
2 + 1/2 cup all-purpose flour
1 cup dark brown sugar
1/2 cup molasses
1/2 tsp. baking soda
2 sticks chopped unsalted butter at room temperature
2 large eggs
1/2 tsp. salt
2 tsp. ground ginger
1 tsp. ground cinnamon
1/2 tsp. ground nutmeg
1/4 tsp. ground cloves
1 cup powdered sugar for dusting

Baking Instructions: Preheat oven to 375f. Beat butter and sugar until light and fluffy and beat in molasses and eggs, one at a time. Mix all dry ingredients in fairly large mixing bowl. Add dry ingredients until well mixed. Line the baking sheet and drop large tablespoons of dough 2 inch apart and bake for 10-12 minutes for chewy and 14-16 minutes for crunchy cookies. Dust with powdered sugar.

Pasta Salads Recipes is a Kindle Italian Pasta Salads Recipes book with 30 heathy tasty Italian pasta salads.

Pasta Cookbook is a Kindle Italian Pasta Recipes book with 30 tasty Italian pasta recipes.

Cupcakes Recipes is a Kindle Cupcakes Cookbook book with 30 tasty cupcakes recipes.

Cookies Cookbook is a Kindle Italian Cookies book with 30 tasty Italian cookies recipes.

Made in the USA
Middletown, DE
19 December 2016